Professor Wooford McPaw's

History of Astronomy

Elliot Kruszynski

Hiya Prof! Ok, let's take a look at what's inside this book.

You see, I first became interested in astronomy as a young pup. I looked up at the stars and thought to myself...

Sorry Prof, we haven't got all the time in the world. Let's get on with it!

EARLY OBSERVERS

Ah, not too much then.

Astronomy is the study of all the objects outside Earth's atmosphere. This includes the sun, moon, planets, stars, galaxies, asteroids and everything else in the universe.

Astronomy is one of the oldest natural sciences. Civilisations in ancient Mesopotamia, Persia, China, India and Greece all examined the night sky. With only the naked eye, they mapped out the stars and used the information they gathered to create calendars, navigate great distances and keep time. The stars told them when to plant their crops and when to harvest them; when the Nile would flood and when to set sail for distant lands.

As early as 5 BC, astronomers concluded that the earth was a sphere.

If the earth was flat, ships would appear on the horizon in one go, rather than appearing gradually.

Yes, and during a lunar eclipse you can see the circular shadow of the earth across the moon.

STONEHENGE 3000 BC

Religious leaders in neolithic cultures lined up circles of stones with the sun and stars to chart the solstices.

The light is coming through the horseshoe. That means it's the longest day of the year.

Time to PARTY!

ANCIENT BABYLON, 1000 BC

Elsewhere, people looked at the night sky and saw shapes that resembled animals and people. They made up stories about what they saw, some of which are still told today.

What if people who were born under certain stars had certain personality traits?

Those stars look like twins, and that one looks like a crab, and this one looks like a centaur.

Sounds bonkers. Let's go with it!

ARISTOTLE

The Ancient Greeks were keen observers of the night sky. They noticed that some points of light stayed steady and appeared in the same place every night. They called these stars. They also noticed that other lights seemed to travel across the sky. They called these 'planets' meaning 'wanderers' in Greek.

Look, Son!

Wish I could wander back to bed...

The entire universe is one great sphere with Earth in its centre.

Around 350 BC, the great Greek philosopher and thinker, Aristotle, came up with a theory.

Little bit arrogant.

The earth and the moon were part of an inner sphere in which four elements (fire, air, water and earth) caused things to be in a state of constant change and movement.

The heavens, which included the stars and planets and everything beyond the moon, were the unchanging realm of the gods.

The stars don't change their relationship to one another. This means that the heavenly sphere is fixed inside a godly substance which I shall call 'quintessence'.

The movement of the planets, comets and everything else in the night sky was put down to the powers of the gods.

PTOLEMY VS. COPERNICUS

In about 140 AD, Claudius Ptolemy, an Alexandrian astronomer, built on the theories of Aristotle. He concluded that the earth was indeed the centre of the universe and that the heavenly bodies orbited the earth in perfect circles.

The earth stands still whilst all the stars and the planets move around it.

How clever.

Oh yes, how wise!

Yay!

This theory, called the geocentric theory, was held to be true for over a thousand years.

In the 16th century, a Polish astronomer and priest called Nicolaus Copernicus came up with a new theory.

From his observations over many years, he concluded that the geocentric model could not be correct, and that rather than the sun orbiting the earth, the earth and the planets orbited the sun.

Furthermore, he worked out that the earth did not stand still, but was constantly spinning on its axis.

This was called the heliocentric model.

From his work as a priest, Copernicus knew how controversial his theory would be. The church still very much believed in Aristotle's idea of a separate heavenly realm in which God went about his business.

What are you up to down there Copernicus?

Nothing to see here, Lord!

Copernicus only allowed his findings to be published after his death, in 1543.

With this tool, Galileo could look at the craters on the moon; he could watch the moons of Jupiter orbiting the planet; he could even see spots on the sun, which moved, proving that the sun also rotated.

No way can you see through those sunglasses.

This confirms without a doubt that Copernicus was correct. The earth and planets revolve around the sun! I shall publish my findings immediately.

What is this dreadful book?

Dialogue Between Two Chief World Systems

How dare he contradict the truth of the Bible! This book even mocks the Pope! Lock him up! Throw away the key!

Galileo spent the rest of his days under house arrest, but he continued his research, writing and inventing.

The four biggest moons of Jupiter (Io, Europa, Ganymede and Callisto) are called the Galilean moons in his honour.

Galileo's theories were soon widely held to be true, raising many new questions in the minds of scientists around the world.

And how does the earth travel around the sun if nothing is pushing it?

When are you two going to buy another drink?

If the earth is always spinning, why don't objects fly off it?

Circles are so last year.

Johannes is so last year.

Around the same time that Galileo invented the telescope, an astronomer called Johannes Kepler noticed that rather than orbiting the sun in circles, the planets moved in oval patterns called ellipses.

In the 1660s, a young English scientist called Isaac Newton tried to work out why this would be the case and came to some fascinating conclusions.

He figured out that there was a force coming from the centre of the earth, drawing objects towards it. He called this force 'gravity' and worked out that the heavier objects are and the closer they are to one another, the more they pull on each other.

Gravity is proportional to the product of masses and inversely proportional to the square of the distance between them.

How compelling...

This answered many of the questions about how and why the planets move the way they do as well as the behaviour of comets, the moon and the tides in the ocean.

So that's why we don't fly off the face of the earth!

New book out now!

Principia: Mathematical Principles of Natural Philosophy

Get them while they're hot!

It was a turning point in scientific thinking.

LEAPS OF IMAGINATION

Newton's findings, along with the improvement of telescope technology, changed the way that humans (and some dogs) looked at our planet.

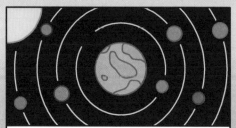

Earth is not the centre of the universe!

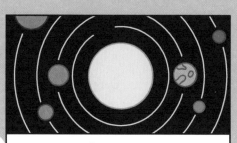

It is one planet among many orbiting the sun.

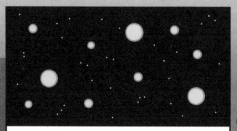

And the sun is just one of billions of stars in the sky, many of which have their own set of planets spinning around them.

Newton's discoveries were so important that he's had a fair few statues erected in his honour, including this one by Eduardo Paolozzi at the British Library in London.

We are nothing but a microscopic speck of dust in an infinite cosmos.

Who knows how many intelligent life forms are out there?

Hopefully more than down here.

This separated a star's radiation into frequencies, allowing astronomers to differentiate between hot, powerful stars and cooler, weaker stars.

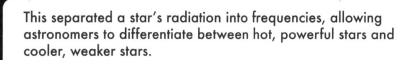

Photography became a useful tool to astronomers, because they could make fine measurements on the images that they captured through the telescope, revealing the sizes and distances between the things they were looking at.

But the most useful tool was, of course, the telescope! We grew ever more sophisticated and ever more powerful.

A TELESCOPIC HISTORY

Early telescopes focu-

Excuse me Prof – I can explain this one! Early telescopes, like the one Galileo invented, focused light using pieces of curved glass called lenses. The bigger the lens, the more powerful the telescope. They were called refracting telescopes.

Perfetto!

Gallileo, 1609

However the glass had to be a precise shape, with not even the tiniest scratch or flaw, otherwise the telescope wouldn't work properly. It was very difficult to manufacture huge, perfect glass lenses. Also, they were very heavy and had a tendency to break.

This is Christian Hugyens' 36 metre long aerial telescope from 1689.

Instead of using a long tube, the main lens was mounted on a tower and the observer stood on the ground with an eyepiece connected to the lens by a string.

EINSTEIN'S THEORY OF RELATIVITY

One such scientist was Albert Einstein. Albert Einstein was born in Germany in 1879.

He grew up to be one of the most clever and famous scientists in history. During his lifetime, Albert Einstein came up with some amazing theories about light, matter, gravity, space and time. His most famous theory was the Theory of Relativity.

Oh wow. Can you explain it to me?

Well... uhhh... It's a bit complicated...

I'll take it from here. I realised that time and distance change, depending on how fast you're moving when you measure them.

So far I'm keeping up.

Whatever, I'm off for a nap.

Time can actually speed up if you're moving slowly through space, or slow down if you're moving quickly.

Ok....

I also realised that mass, or the total amount of stuff in an object, can change depending on the speed of the object. If you started moving very fast, you would actually have more mass than you do right now.

My head feels quite heavy now....

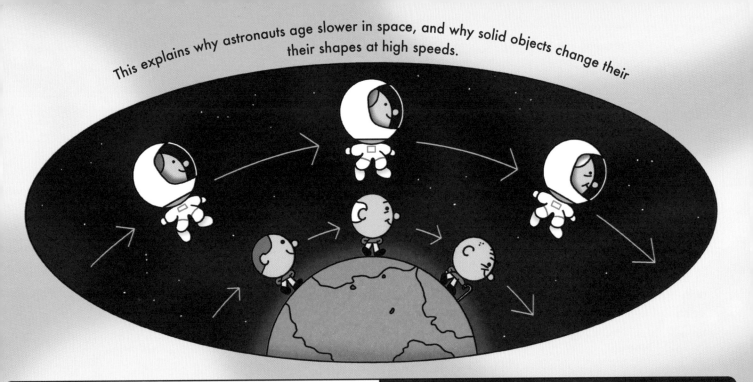

However, light always travels at a constant speed, regardless of how fast you're moving when you measure it.

The speed of light is 300,000 kilometres per second. Nothing could ever move as quickly as the speed of light.

The Theory of Relativity explores how space and time are connected to one another in relation to the speed of light.

Blimey...

Energy equals mass times the speed of light, squared: $E=mc^2$. This means that energy and mass are different forms of the same thing.

Einstein also expanded on Newton's theories of gravity. He said that gravity has the power to twist space-time. The more mass an object has, the more its gravity warps the space-time around it.

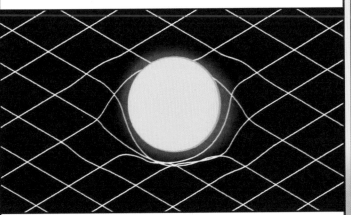

So a really massive body like the sun bends the fabric of the universe around it, like a heavy ball resting on a stretched sheet of rubber.

Mind bending AND space bending! Now do you understand?

Not at all...

THE SPACE RACE

Einstein's discoveries paved the way to many important developments, one of which was nuclear power. Under the right conditions, atoms can split apart in a process called 'fission' which converts the mass of the original atoms into energy.

USA

RUSSIA

After the Second World War, Russia and America entered into a race to develop powerful nuclear weapons.

I have the bigger missile.

No mine is bigger!

When they had raced each other to a standstill, they turned their attention to space, using some of their new technologies to propel rockets outside of the earth's atmosphere.

We will reach the moon first.

No we will!

North American Space Agency (NASA)

Russian Space Agency (SSSR)

Over the course of 20 years, many ground-breaking advancements were made.

Grrrr.....

We win!

1957 Russia's satellite, Sputnik 1, is launched into space.

We win again!

1961 Russian astronaut Yuri Gagarin orbits the earth.

ARGH!

And again!

1963 Russian astronaut Valentina Tereshkova spends three days in space, orbiting the earth 48 times.

AARRRRGHHHH!!!!

Take that!

1966 The Russian space probe, Venera 3, is the first man-made object to enter the atmosphere of another planet.

Wait... WHAT?

1969 American astronauts walk on the moon.

On the way to the launchpad in April 1961, Yuri Gagarin asked the bus driver to stop and he had a wee on the rear right-hand tyre of the bus. Since then, all astronauts going into space do the same. Female astronauts take a vial of urine to splash against the tyre.

SPACE PROBES

It costs a lot of money and it is very high risk to send people into space. From the 1970s onwards, space programmes began moving their focus from astronauts to space probes.

A space probe is an unmanned robotic spacecraft. It is equipped with a set of scientific instruments that the probe uses to gather data and transmit it back to Earth.

Different types of space probes were designed and engineered for different purposes.

Rovers/landers were designed to land on planets or asteroids to collect information about the terrain. They take samples of dust, soil and rocks and send back detailed photos of the landscape. The Mars Exploration Rover, Opportunity, was active from 2003 to 2018, sending back a treasure trove of information about the planet.

Interplanetary probes fly past celestial bodies and keep going. Voyager 1 is the most famous interplanetary space probe. Launched in 1977, it has travelled 17 billion kilometres in 45 years. It flew past Jupiter and Saturn and sent back detailed images of their moons. It is now beyond the solar system in interplanetary space.

Orbiters orbit a celestial body in order to observe it for a number of years. The Magellan probe, launched by NASA in 1989, mapped the entire surface of Venus during its five years in orbit.

Space probes are more cost-effective and less dangerous than manned space missions.

But humans can do things that robots can't, like setting up scientific equipment in a more exact and useful way. So don't rule us out just yet!

OUR SOLAR SYSTEM

The solar system is our little neighbourhood of planets revolving around the sun, our special star. Because we can observe it more closely, we know much more about this neighbourhood than we do about the rest of the universe.

Sun: The sun contains 99 percent of the solar system's total mass. It is about a million times the size of Earth and 1,000 times the size of Jupiter. That's why it has such a strong gravitational pull.

Our solar system includes eight planets, 170 moons, five dwarf planets and millions of asteroids and comets. The solar system formed around 4.5 billion years ago, and it measures two light years into space.

What is a light year?

A light year is the distance light travels in one year. About 9.5 trillion kilometres.

Mercury: A tiny, dense planet, close to the sun. Temperatures on its surface reach 430° C during the day but are freezing at night because the atmosphere is so thin, all the heat escapes.

Venus: The second brightest object in the night sky, after the moon. It is a similar size and density to Earth, but it cannot sustain life. Powerful winds of 720 kph blast across a surface that is hotter than an oven.

Earth: The only planet known to support life. It has an atmosphere rich in oxygen and plenty of water on its surface.

Mars: About half the size of Earth, Mars is cold and dry with a thin atmosphere and weak gravity. The iron oxide in its soil gives the planet a reddish colour.

Mercury, Venus, Earth and Mars are small and rocky. They are called the inner planets. Between Mars and Jupiter lies a vast asteroid belt. The planets on the other side are much bigger but less dense, with liquid cores and gaseous outer layers. They are called the outer planets.

Jupiter: Jupiter accounts for twice the mass of all the other planets combined. It's about 1,300 times the size of Earth.

Saturn: The second largest planet, Saturn, is the most distant planet we can see without a telescope. It is surrounded by six rings made up of dust, rocks and chunks of ice.

Uranus and Neptune: Known as the ice giants, these distant planets are blue because of the methane gas in their atmospheres. Uranus is tilted on its side, so that its equator is at right angles to its orbit. This means that it has 21 years of sunlight during its summer and 21 years of darkness in its winter. Scientists think it might have been knocked over by a massive object at some point in its distant history.

Pluto: Beyond Neptune lies Pluto, which was once thought of as a planet, but is now considered a dwarf planet because of its small size and weak gravity.

25

THE HUBBLE TELESCOPE

One of the things that makes Earth such a special planet is its atmosphere. Clouds and gasses create a protective blanket around the earth so that it never gets too hot or too cold. However, those same clouds and gasses block the view of space, limiting astronomers' ability to gather data.

In the 1970s, scientists at NASA began developing a giant telescope that would orbit outside Earth's atmosphere, providing a crystal-clear view of everything beyond our planet.

Far out!

In 1990, they succeeded. The Hubble Space Telescope is a reflecting telescope that orbits around 600 km above Earth.

It has a 2.4 metre primary mirror, as well as other instruments that gather information about chemical compositions and light emissions from far distant objects.

It also has a camera that can take images 10 times clearer than those of the largest Earth-based telescope.

My computer communicates with satellites that tell the Hubble what to do. The Hubble communicates back to me through those satellites.

The Hubble is about the size of a double decker bus!

Cool!

Isn't she a beauty?

The Hubble has been key to countless important astronomical discoveries. It has found new planetary systems, emerging galaxies and massive black holes. It has revealed Pluto's moon and allowed us to look at objects that are more than 13.4 billion light years away from our planet.

The James Webb Space Telescope (JWST) is a new, even more powerful telescope that works alongside the Hubble. Launched in 2021, the JWST uses a primary mirror that is folded into 18 hexagonal segments that open up to become one vast mirror with a diameter of 6.5 metres!

— Great design!

It is so powerful it can look out into the earliest, most distant galaxies, helping us find clues about the very beginning of space and time.

Amongst other things, the Hubble has helped us understand how galaxies work.

Most of the universe's objects are located in galaxies. These are huge groups of stars, gas and dust held together by gravitational attraction. For many years it was not known what caused such a powerful gravitational field, but now it is understood that most large galaxies have a supermassive black hole at their centre, which pulls all the stars and gasses into its orbit.

Earth is located in a galaxy called the Milky Way. At its centre is a supermassive black hole called Sagittarius A•, which contains as much mass as four million suns.

The Milky Way is a spiral galaxy, which takes the shape of a flat spinning disk, with arms coming out of a central bulge.

Let's take a look at some of the different types of galaxies.

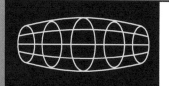

Elliptical galaxies look like giant cigars. They contain older stars.

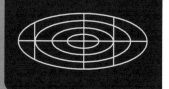

Lenticular galaxies are flat and round, like a spiral galaxy, but without the extending arms.

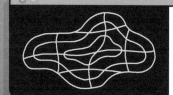

Irregular galaxies are strange shapes, because they are often close to other galaxies with strong gravitational fields.

The word galaxy comes from the Greek word for 'milk', *galaxia*, because from Earth, our galaxy looks like a splash of milk across the sky.

Most galaxies are dwarf galaxies. They also take the shape of elliptical, spiral or lenticular galaxies, but they are much smaller – about a hundredth the size of the Milky Way, with only a billion or so stars.

A billion? Pah – that's nothing!

Dwarf galaxies usually orbit a larger galaxy. The Milky Way has at least a dozen dwarf galaxies orbiting it. Eventually, some these dwarf galaxies will be cannibalised by the Milky Way.

Cannibalised? Yipes!

When a small galaxy merges with a big galaxy, the big galaxy stays as it is whilst the smaller one is torn apart.

Yum! Yum!

The Milky Way is part of a cluster of 45 galaxies. The Andromeda galaxy is our largest galactic neighbour, almost three times the size of the Milky Way. It could be that in a few billion years the Milky Way will collide with Andromeda to form one huge galaxy.

Oh dear.

Looking tasty!

LIFE CYCLE OF A STAR

So a galaxy contains billions of stars...

But what exactly IS a star?

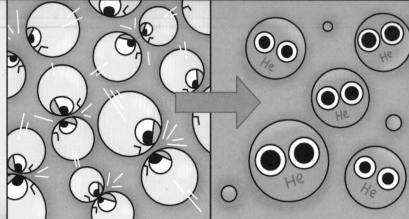

A star is a giant ball of plasma (very hot gas) held together by gravity. Inside the star's core, parts of hydrogen atoms crash into each other, creating helium nuclei. This process is called nuclear fusion, and the energy it releases makes stars shine.

So how are they formed?

These enormous clouds are constantly swirling about. Sometimes the gas and dust starts to build up in a certain part of the nebula. When it becomes quite dense, this area begins to collapse in on itself, drawn inwards by its own gravity, becoming ever denser and hotter as it contracts.

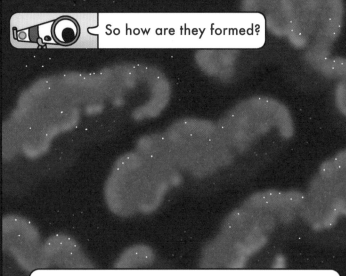

A galaxy contains not only billions of stars, but also vast clouds of gas and dust called nebulae. A single nebula can be as big as our solar system.

It's called a pre-stellar core.

When the temperature at the core reaches 10 million° C, nuclear fusion starts to happen and a star is born.

There are all different types of stars. The biggest ones are called supergiants. They are around 100 times the size of the sun and they glow red or orange. The most common stars are called red dwarfs. They are much cooler and smaller; only a tenth of the size of the sun.

RED DWARF

Once a star has used up all its nuclear fuel, it begins to die. An average sized star will swell up to become a 'red giant', and then start shedding its outer layers. The star's core remains as a 'white dwarf', which cools off over billions of years, fading and changing colour as it does so.

WHITE DWARF

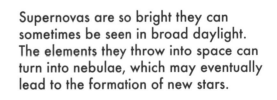

Supergiant stars die a more dramatic death. When they have burned all their nuclear fuel, their core collapses causing runaway nuclear fusion in a massive explosion called a

SUPERNOVA

Supernovas are so bright they can sometimes be seen in broad daylight. The elements they throw into space can turn into nebulae, which may eventually lead to the formation of new stars.

STEPHEN HAWKING

Stephen Hawking is probably the most famous scientist of the last 50 years. He had a terrible disease that left him unable to move, but nonetheless he came up with some brilliant ideas about how the universe works.

Hello

Building on the work of Einstein and exploring the new information that was coming in about the behaviour of stars and galaxies, Hawking asked questions about why the universe behaves in the way it does.

Hawking's first breakthrough was proving the Big Bang theory. In the 1960s, it was known that the universe was continually expanding, but it was not clear why.

WHYYYYYYY

One theory, called the Steady State theory, proposed that the universe has been expanding forever, with new matter being added to it all the time.

The Big Bang theory, on the other hand, stated that the universe did not always exist in the way that we know it, but rather it was once very, very tiny. So tiny it could fit into a single point, a fraction of the size of an atom. This point was called 'singularity'.

Around 13 billion years ago this micro-universe exploded into being with a BIG BANG, shooting matter across time and space and cooling as it spread.

Hawking used mathematics to prove that the Steady State theory could not possibly be right, and that even though it boggles the imagination, the Big Bang theory was correct.

Another theory that Hawking came up with, which hasn't yet been proven is that perhaps our universe is just one of many universes. This 'multiverse' would look like a bubbly foam, with each bubble containing a universe that may be very similar or completely different to ours.

BLACK HOLES

Stephen Hawking came up with lots of other theories about the fabric of the universe. One of them was about black holes, something which we know very little about.

That's not very helpful, Professor...

Quiet you! A black hole is a region of space where matter has collapsed in on itself, creating a huge amount of mass concentrated in a very small area! How's that?

Hey let me out!

The gravitational pull of this region is so strong that not even light can escape, making them totally invisible.

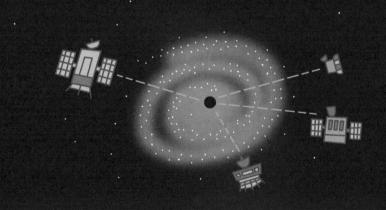

Although a black hole cannot be seen, astronomers can use special instruments to observe the behaviour of the dust, stars and galaxies, which swirl around them like a whirlpool, getting hotter and hotter the closer they get to the black hole.

Objects that fall into black holes are literally stretched to breaking point, pulled apart by the overpowering gravity

Black holes come in different sizes. The most common type is the stellar black hole. These are formed when a supergiant star ends its life in a supernova (see p. 31). What is left of the star, which is still around 10 times the mass of the sun, collapses into an area only a few kilometres across. Astronomers believe that there are dozens of stellar black holes in the Milky Way.

Supergiant → Supernova → Stellar black hole

Will the sun ever collapse and turn into a black hole?

No, it's not big enough. Now let's catch these rays.

Galaxy

Black hole

Supermassive black holes are the biggest of all. They have a mass greater than the combination of one million suns. Scientists believe that every large galaxy has a supermassive black hole at its centre.

Hawking did a lot of research into what happens to matter that is drawn into a black hole, and also about the energy that is emitted from the surface of a black hole. He believed that there are microscopic black holes called primordial black holes dotted all over the universe, which have existed since the universe began.

Primordial black holes are the size of a single atom, yet contain the mass of a huge mountain.

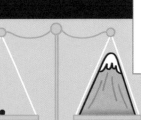

Hawking's theories about black holes are still being explored.

DARK MATTER

Everything we see in the sky – stars, planets, asteroids, dust, gas… is only a small fraction of what the universe is made up of. Most of the universe – some say 85% of it – is made up of dark matter and dark energy.

What is that??

Dark matter is one of the universe's greatest mysteries. We know a lot about what it's not, but not what it is.

Right so what *isn't* it?

Dark matter is NOT made of atoms.

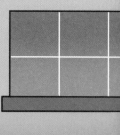

Ok.

It does not reflect light.

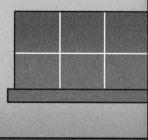

Yes, and...

It does not release electromagnetic radiation.

Uh huh...

However, it DOES have gravity, which is how we know that it exists.

Oh, well that's helpful.

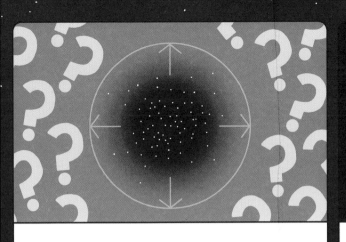

Dark energy is an even bigger mystery. Something is making the universe expand at an ever increasing rate.

That something is creating enough gravitational pull to bend the starlight of distant galaxies. It is also contributing to the gravity that holds galaxies together, which would otherwise be spinning at speeds too high to stay in one piece.

It seems the keys to the universe are locked in this dark matter and dark energy. Using computers and satellites, scientists are creating models with which to gather dark matter data.

Various theories have been put forward. Some believe that dark matter is made of objects that we know about, such as cold gasses, black holes and dark galaxies.

Others believe that dark matter may be made of strange particles from the early days of the universe, which behave in ways that we don't yet understand.

INTERNATIONAL SPACE STATION

Some of the research into dark matter is being carried out on the International Space Station, or ISS.

The ISS is a space research laboratory that orbits the earth. It is the largest artificial object in space and the third brightest object in the night sky. 16 countries worked together to build the ISS. The first component was launched in 1998, and since then it has been added to and improved many times.

The ISS looks like a giant dragonfly. The central pole is called the truss. It is made of lots of modules where astronauts can live and work for months at a time.

Coming off the truss are 16 huge solar panels that power the space station.

Crews of three people stay on the ISS for periods of three to six months. They must bring or produce all the air, water and food they need to survive for that period.

DOES LIFE EXIST ELSEWHERE?

This is a question that astronomers have been asking since back in the days of Ancient Greece. Life as we know it needs very specific conditions to support it, and intelligent life needs even more specific conditions.

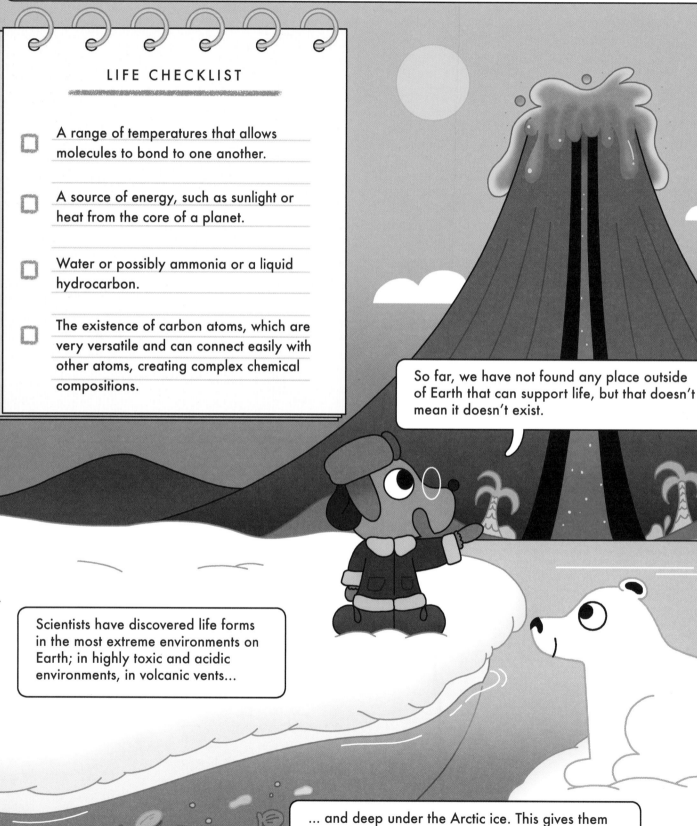

LIFE CHECKLIST

☐ A range of temperatures that allows molecules to bond to one another.

☐ A source of energy, such as sunlight or heat from the core of a planet.

☐ Water or possibly ammonia or a liquid hydrocarbon.

☐ The existence of carbon atoms, which are very versatile and can connect easily with other atoms, creating complex chemical compositions.

So far, we have not found any place outside of Earth that can support life, but that doesn't mean it doesn't exist.

Scientists have discovered life forms in the most extreme environments on Earth; in highly toxic and acidic environments, in volcanic vents...

... and deep under the Arctic ice. This gives them hope that it might be possible for life to exist in inhospitable environments on other planets.

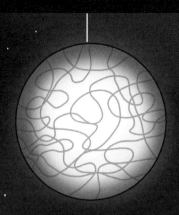

Europa is covered in ice, but there are hot, hydrothermal vents feeding a liquid ocean beneath the crust, and perhaps primitive forms of life could exist in such an environment.

In the solar system, the most likely location for extraterrestrial life is one of Jupiter's 63 moons, Europa.

Titan, Saturn's largest moon, is also a contender. It is far from the sun, but has a hot core that might allow alien life to survive deep underground.

Beyond our solar system, we can only imagine what planets and life forms might exist. Scientists including Carl Sagan and Stephen Hawking believed that it was unlikely that life DIDN'T exist elsewhere.

Studies of meteorites on Earth have found that they carry fragments of DNA, the key building block of life. If cosmic dust can carry DNA across galaxies, it may explain how life evolved so quickly on Earth, and perhaps the same could occur on other planets with the right conditions.

So the answer is probably!

Astronomers have suggested that there could be as many as 11 billion Earth-sized planets orbiting Sun-sized stars that could be home to alien life forms. The nearest such planet may be a mere 12 light years away.

WHAT DOES THE FUTURE HOLD?

There are great advancements being made in the fields of space science, astronomy and astrophysics as scientists try to overcome the many obstacles that stand between us tiny dogs (and humans) and the great mysteries of the universe.

Space agencies like NASA are developing new technologies that will allow robotic probes to travel efficiently beyond our solar system. Micro satellites will be smaller, cheaper and more efficient and will convey data from the probes back to Earth.

New systems of rocket propulsion and navigation are being explored, which will allow us to launch into space more easily and safely.

Astronomers have access to ever more sophisticated technologies to help them in their research. Telescopes like the new James Webb Space Telescope will allow them to look at ancient galaxies to discover more about the origins of the universe and the mysteries of dark energy and dark matter.

Mathematicians and physicists build on the theories of Einstein and Hawking to work out how and why elements of the universe behave the way they do.

The resources of space are also being explored. If we could mine valuable minerals from asteroids and move our polluting industries off the earth, we could reduce the emissions on Earth and maybe avoid planetary disaster. Space X is a private company that has developed a reusable rocket that could make space colonisation a more realistic possibility.

When we think about the future of astronomy, the possibilities really are endless!

And what about space tourism?

Hmm... I think we have more important things to think about.

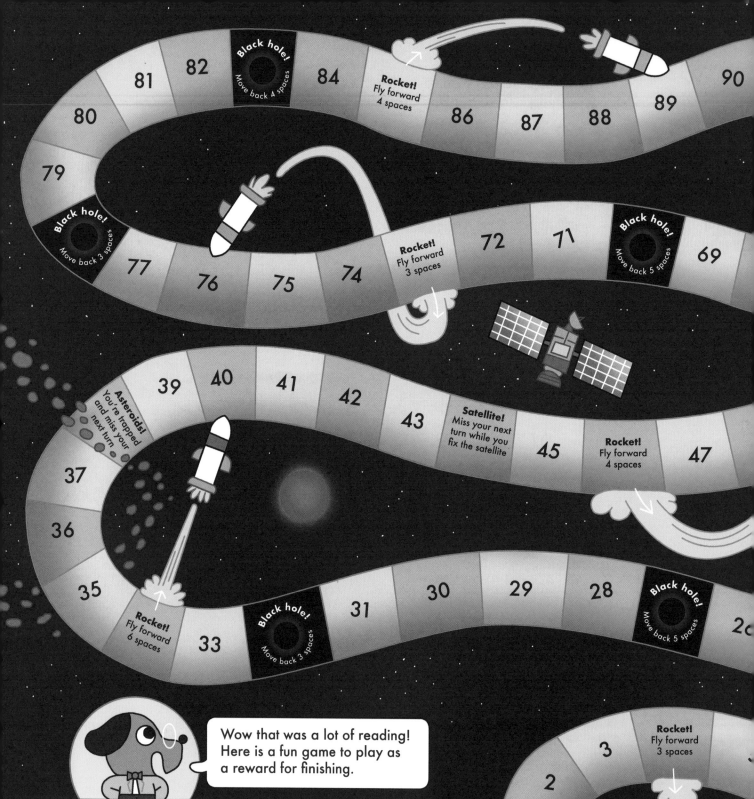

81 82 84 80 79 77 76 75 74 72 71 69

Black hole! Move back 4 spaces

Rocket! Fly forward 4 spaces

86 87 88 89 90

Black hole! Move back 3 spaces

Rocket! Fly forward 3 spaces

Black hole! Move back 5 spaces

Asteroids! You're trapped and miss your next turn

39 40 41 42 43 45 47 37 36 35 33 31 30 29 28

Satellite! Miss your next turn while you fix the satellite

Rocket! Fly forward 4 spaces

Rocket! Fly forward 6 spaces

Black hole! Move back 3 spaces

Black hole! Move back 5 spaces

2

Wow that was a lot of reading! Here is a fun game to play as a reward for finishing.

1 2 3

Rocket! Fly forward 3 spaces

RACE TO EARTH!

The rules are simple; you can have as many players as you want. To play you'll need a die and a counter for each player (this can be anything small like a button or coin). All players start on GO and must take turns rolling and moving their counter the number on the die.

The youngest player gets to go first and the first player to reach Earth wins!

GO

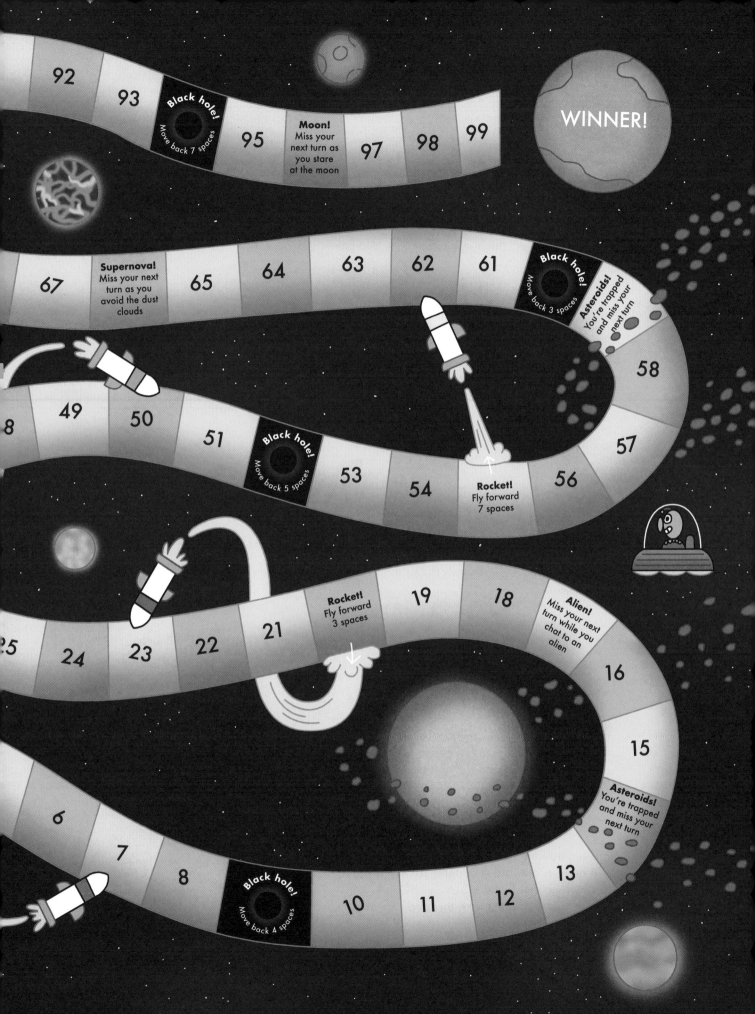

92 93 **Black hole!** Move back 7 spaces 95 **Moon!** Miss your next turn as you stare at the moon 97 98 99

WINNER!

67 **Supernova!** Miss your next turn as you avoid the dust clouds 65 64 63 62 61 **Black hole!** Move back 3 spaces **Asteroids!** You're trapped and miss your next turn 58

8 49 50 51 **Black hole!** Move back 5 spaces 53 54 **Rocket!** Fly forward 7 spaces 56 57

25 24 23 22 21 **Rocket!** Fly forward 3 spaces 19 18 **Alien!** Miss your next turn while you chat to an alien 16 15

6 7 8 **Black hole!** Move back 4 spaces 10 11 12 13 **Asteroids!** You're trapped and miss your next turn

Hey! In case you fine readers forget anything that's in the book, use this glossary to help remember what's what.

Black hole

A region of space-time where gravity is so strong that nothing — no particles or even light — can escape from it.

Dark matter

A form of matter that makes up 85% of the universe, but which does not obey the laws of physics as we understand them. It may be made up of sub-atomic particles that we don't yet know about.

Europa

The smallest of the four Galilean moons orbiting Jupiter. It has a very smooth surface that leads scientists to believe that a water ocean exists beneath the crust, which could possibly harbour extra-terrestrial life.

Gagarin, Yuri

A Russian cosmonaut and the first person to journey into outer space, completing an orbit of the earth in 1961.

Geocentric model

The theory that stated that the earth is in the centre of the universe and the sun and other bodies revolve around it.

Gravity

A phenomenon by which all things with energy and mass, including planets, stars and even light, are attracted to one another.

Heliocentric model

The theory that stated that the sun is at the centre of the universe and that the planets and other bodies revolve around it.

Herschel's telescope

Built in 1789, and known as the Great 40-Foot Telescope, this reflecting telescope had a 120 cm primary mirror and was the biggest telescope in the world for 50 years.

Hubble telescope

A space telescope launched in 1990, which orbits the earth, gathering data and images and sending them back for analysis. With its 2.4 m mirror and its clear view of space from outside the atmosphere, it remains one of the most useful astronomical tools today.

James Webb Space Telescope (JWST)

A space telescope launched in 2021 with a mirror made of hexagonal segments that open up to create a huge 6.5 m primary mirror. This allows it to detect objects that are too old and faint for the Hubble, providing information about the origins of the universe.

Nebula

A vast interstellar cloud of dust and gas. It is usually formed from the explosion of a dying star in a supernova, and it is where new stars are born.

Neutron star

The collapsed core of a supergiant star, which is left over after a supernova. A neutron star has a radius of only 10 km but almost twice the mass of the sun. They are the smallest and densest objects we know of.

Planet	An astronomical body that is massive enough to be rounded by its own gravity and which orbits a star.
Plasma	The superheated matter that stars are made of. It is so hot that the electrons are ripped away from the atoms, forming an ionized gas.
Principia	A book by Isaac Newton published in 1687 that explains the physical laws of motion and gravity. It marked a turning point in the history of science.
Reflecting telescope	A telescope that uses curved mirrors to gather light and magnify far away objects.
Refracting telescope	A telescope which, like binoculars, uses perfect curved lenses made of glass to magnify far away objects.
Space probe	A robotic spacecraft that travels through space, orbiting, landing or flying past planetary bodies and gathering information about them.
Space Race	A 20th century competition between the Soviet Union and the United States to achieve domination in space.
Space X	A US-based private corporation founded by Elon Musk with the goal of developing space transport and enabling the colonisation of Mars.
Spectroscope	An instrument that separates light by wavelength, allowing astronomers to analyse the chemical makeup of stars.
Sputnik 1	The first human object to be launched into space, this Russian satellite orbited the earth for three weeks in 1957 before its batteries ran out. It sparked the great Space Race and all the developments that followed.
Star	An astronomical body that is a sphere of plasma held together by its own gravity, producing light and heat from the nuclear fusion inside its core.
Supernova	A powerful explosion that occurs when a supergiant star dies. As its core collapses, its temperature rises, triggering runaway nuclear fusion and releasing gravitational potential energy in a massive bang.
Tereshkova, Valentina	A Soviet cosmonaut who orbited the earth 48 times in 1963.
Theory of Relativity	Two connected theories by Albert Einstein explaining how speed affects mass, time and space and how gravity behaves.
Titan	The largest moon of Saturn, Titan is the only place besides Earth known to have rivers, lakes and seas on its surface. Its thick atmosphere is rich in carbon compounds, meaning that it could possibly harbour life.
Venera space probes	Russian probes designed to gather information about Venus. Venera 7 was the first probe to touch down on another planet (1970). Venera 9 sent back images from the planet's surface (1975).

Professor Wooford McPaw's History of Astronomy

Text © Ziggy Hanaor and Elliot Kruszynski
Illustration © Elliot Kruszynski

British Library Cataloguing-in-Publication Data.

A CIP record for this book is available from the British Library
ISBN: 978-1-80066-023-6

First published in 2022

Cicada Books Ltd
48 Burghley Road
London, NW5 1UE
www.cicadabooks.co.uk

Printed in Poland